Early Mourning

Anju Mariya Babu V

All India Forum for English Students, Scholars, and Trainers (AIFEST)

Early Mourning
Anju Mariya Babu V
First Published: December 2023
Published by
All India Forum for English Students, Scholars,
and Trainers (AIFEST)

Indian Print Edition Distribution
Amazon, Flipkart

Copyright 2023 © Anju Mariya Babu V
This book remains the copyrighted property of the author. No part of
the book may be reproduced or transmitted for commercial or
non-commercial purposes without prior written permission from the
author.

International Distribution
Smashwords, Inc., Los Gatos, USA

Introduction

Early Mourning, the debut poetry collection by Anju Mariya – one of the most promising young litterateurs from South India – is a poetic testament to the transformative power of words in the face of life's harshest adversities. In this anthology, Mariya's poetic voice emerges as a gentle yet resonant melody, crafting verses that bridge the chasm between the personal and the universal, the realistic and the imaginary. Themes ranging from loss and memory to love and resilience, weave together a collection that transcends the ordinary and touches the very essence of the human soul.

These verses offer solace to those who have known the pain of loss, reminding us that in the darkest hours, the magic of words can illuminate the profoundest grief. The titular poem explores the profound theme of loss, capturing the heart-wrenching moment of parting with astonishing precision. The lines, "It's too early to say goodbye / Without losing hope," embody the tug-of-war between despair and resilience, as she navigates the treacherous waters of grief. The use of "early mourning" not only plays on the dual meaning of 'morning' but also evokes a sense of premature sorrow, as if the very universe mourns with her.

The poem "Our Stories" sets the tone for this enchanting poetic journey, highlighting the importance of preserving our own narratives and celebrating the uniqueness of individual experiences. As the collection unfolds, Mariya invites readers to ponder the complexities of love and loss, the transformative power of love, the need for belonging, the significance of trust, and the impact of societal prejudice. She navigates the seasons of life and delves into the nuances of aging, resilience, and the pursuit of purpose.

Mariya's ability to translate personal sorrow into universal resonance is a recurring theme throughout the collection. In "Living with Ghosts," she explores the haunting persistence of memories, emphasizing the inescapable nature of certain recollections, which, like ghosts, linger in the recesses of our consciousness. "Far Away #Home" delves into the yearning for a distant sense of home, mirroring the universal quest for self-acceptance and healing.

Throughout the collection, the poetic symphony in her verses serves as a perfect foil to the cacophony of emotions within. She employs metaphors and vivid imagery that paint a sensory experience for the reader, allowing them to immerse themselves fully in the emotional landscapes she portrays. For instance, in "Wreckage," she encapsulates resilience in the face of adversity, comparing the heart to a "home with four chambers" that can withstand wreckage.

Yet, Mariya doesn't shy away from exploring the darker facets of the human experience. "Shame" delves into the corrosive nature of self-doubt, while "Choking Under the Voices" confronts the haunting impact of humiliation and self-doubt. The melancholic mood protracts further in the pervading darkness of "Melancholia," the weeping hearts wandering near desolate valleys in "Forsaken," and the impassioned exploration of cathartic suffering in "Mourning," culminating in the finality of letting go in "Burial" and "Buried Pangs".

As the collection progresses, the author continues to delve into complex emotions and experiences, such as the fragmentary nature of memory in "Fragmented Piece of Word" and the transformative power of catharsis in "Confession." Her words are not only beautiful but also thought-provoking, challenging readers to introspect and reflect on their own experiences.

In "Toxic Positivity," Mariya takes an unconventional approach, portraying positivity as unable to save a heart from wreckage, challenging the notion that relentless optimism can always mend wounds. She offers a balanced perspective on the complexities of emotions and the limitations of trying to "stay positive" at all costs. Lines like "Living in half-dead memories / Like a ghost, / Wandering in the graveyards." create a haunting refrain that emphasizes the spectral nature of the past. "A Poem on Grief and Love" tenderly unites love and loss, weaving them into narratives that endure: Delving into the unspoken sentiments that weigh upon the heart, "Unsaid" reminds us of the consequences of silence: "Some words float, / on the surface of memory."

Mariya's collection reaches its pinnacle in poems like "Battle Field," where she offers a poignant promise of support and refuge amidst chaos, "Slaughtered Thoughts," which delves into the inner battle of dealing with intrusive and negative thoughts, and "Stains of Stigma" which paints a harrowing picture of prejudice, where souls are left stained with the weight of societal biases. She dwells on spirituality and resilience in the meditative pieces "Holding on" and "On Patience". The latter offers a mystical perspective on suffering as the price to pay for connecting with the divine. Her enigmatic language adds a layer of depth to the poems, inviting readers to contemplate the relationship between patience and spirituality.

In the final poem, "Exit," Mariya offers a sense of closure and acceptance, reinforcing the idea that despite all the exits in life, our existence remains unshaken: The repeated affirmation "I exist, I exist, I exist" serve as a powerful declaration of presence and selfhood.

Each poem in this collection is a fragment of the human soul, illuminated with lyrical finesse and profound introspection. This volume offers experiences that will linger long after the last page is turned, leading to the realization that mourning, like poetry itself, is a means to transcend life's darkest moments. *Early Mourning* is more than a collection of poems; it is a lyrical journey into the heart of the human experience.

Aifest Editorial Team

Table of Contents

Our Stories

What makes us unique?
Our stories,
rooted in memories
that failed to fade away.
Our choices
that were once close to our hearts.
Our truths,
that lingered too long with us.
The sorrows that we carried so far.
Our unexpressed thoughts, feelings,
and those unsaid words.
Twists and turns, which were part of our journey.
Those deep voyages, where we met our ghosts.
And those pangs of pain that we swallowed.
Then our buried stories will slowly take form.
And we preserve our ghosts,
By writing in an unknown language.
Gradually rendering our secret stories,
We live our extraordinary lives.

Living with Ghosts

Prologue

'Don't take things too seriously', they say
    What if it still haunts you? Bury it alive,
    The one that consumed your waking days!
    And lend it a burial – ceremonial and ritualistic.
    POV: Let's talk about pathological reminiscences
    and living with ghosts.
    When you grow strange to yourself,
    slowly the 'stranger' in you will awake.
    Your entire life will become a waking nightmare.
    There are moments, when you bleed inside-out
    not knowing,
    when the last drop will ooze out and drain you dry.
    These are those scars, that will remain forever.
    And incurable with time.
    Still, like a thorn, will cause you to bleed.
    Then you will build a coffin, and after reciting
    the ceremonial prayers, will close and seal it.
    To bury in the depths of the sea.
    Because you know, if you open it again,
    you have to live with that haunting body again.
    Now you know, you will start to live with ghosts
    raised from the buried body.
    Because you have buried it alive.
    And now, accursed to live with ghosts.

Epilogue

I know, writing will save one from heart wreckage,
   It's safer to bleed on the page with words than alone!

Early Mourning
It's too early to say goodbye
Without losing hope.
While parting,
those few words can break you apart.
Slowly dissolving into tears
Fading away without
Any trace in this early morning.
When your life has come to grief
Nothing will bring you back ashore.
In this early mourning,
It's too late to whisper adieu.
A small valediction,
And it's not enough!
To cover the heartache...
Oh! In this mourning
While griever bemoans the loss
Little by little, this melancholic heart
Slips into despair.
Without mourning the early death.

Far Away #Home
Choking and crying
shouting and struggling
yes, I am yearning for a #home,
that is far from my heart.
Near the glass, I am searching
All the views from a bell jar
Made my world more chaotic
And I am trying to strangle
the sobbing soul.
All I need is a #home,
that is far beyond the reach
of my old memories.
A far away #home
where I can bleed secretly
where I can heal secretly
where I can listen to my wounded self.
There, I will embrace myself,
for all my imperfections and weaknesses.
Yes, I need a faraway #home
to linger a little more
on my inner secrets.
There I will meet my raw naked self
It was too scared
to appear in front of my mirror,
where I look every day.
A far away #home
to find my dearest self again...
To share, to shout
all the choking truths to the mountains.

Leaving Behind
At every knocking,
She unknowingly
Hastens her steps
Without asking questions
She opens the door.
Now, a decade has gone...
Still waiting,
For the one who she longs for, for years.
Feels too lonely in a home
Where time is just a metaphor for living.
Without knowing,
Its meaning
Lost in foregone days.
And travelling to an unknown future.
By rendering unsung stories.
Every similar face
Every similar voice,
Leaves something deep to discover.
And she lives,
Leaving memories behind the door.

6

Home Coming
On a winter day,
He was alone.
Wandering the wilds
Suddenly started a light snowfall.
Too lost and tiresome
He looked to the high
And started to talk
But the sky was empty.
He was away from home
Too far to be found,
Living in half-dead memories
Like a ghost,
Wandering in the graveyards.
Half-forgotten, half-dead,
Memories haunt him terribly.
He was utterly quiet.
Pangs of guilt hit him hard
He was too terrified.
Image of his beloved slowly
Appeared in his mind
He felt relieved and surprised
He was not dead.
When the dead soul's dance was over,
His angst came to an end
And he lamented on his half-love.
While searching the lost path,
There waited his beloved.
When he saw her from far,
His heart throbbed
And he found his way home.

Melancholia
Darkness is brooding everywhere,
a pair of large, mournful eyes.
Oh! this haunting melancholy
is creeping slowly,
with dreadful thoughts.
Surrounded by the sombre air
Unable to breathe
Now, in low spirits...
Floating continuously
Where the straightway was lost
Lost in airless spaces...
Lost in the melancholic mood.

Mourning
When last night's lost thoughts
strike with painful angst,
I was terrified, and shivered with
hopeless cries.
And lamented over and over in
narrow spaces,
Oh! A terrible beauty was born.
My mourning has been completed,
and the ceremony was over!

Nowhere to be Found

For all the people
I have lost somewhere.
Yes, there are many beautiful faces
I can still remember.
A few helping hands,
I still recall.
We met while passing,
each other's crossroads.
I heard somewhere,
'A new friend is a new journey to begin'.
And we started our rollercoaster ride
through each other's destiny.
When our predestined days ended,
I lost many beloved faces.
Yes, I lost, much loved ones.
My heart now knows,
I lost them utterly.
These were my people,
I have lost somewhere
And now nowhere to be found.

Shame
The burden of scorn,
that I carried.
Self in others' eyes
Core experience of
an alien among others.
Self, diffused and dissolved
in the spell of eyes.
Mind filled with contempt and disdain
Stories were created with derision
Jeering voices vibrated everywhere
Sneering remarks shattered one's image
Taunting comments felt like
a sudden slap on the face.
Stains of stigma lingered on
too long in the heart
Resulting in loathing oneself.

The Places, I Don't Belong to
It was sheer disapproval
A complete rejection.
When I entered,
There started long admonishing talks.
Among them,
I found many rebuking faces.
While alone in the strangeness,
I could only sense wry smiles
And chastising looks.

Tonight

Tonight, I will remember you.
Like wild embers dying slowly,
reminiscences of past will fade little by little.
Our story will dissolve in wild tears
And I will walk down the memory lane.
Nothing left,
there is nothing to write.
Only ashes of bygone love,
from the days of yore.
Yes, tonight I will remember you!

Wreckage
It all started with a doubt
a pain growing from the core of the heart.
Moving slowly, against all odds,
despite the heartache...
Isn't it hard?
When you break apart,
some pieces are still there,
to remind, it is not the end.
At the end of the tunnel,
you will again find light.
When you burn inside-out,
darling, don't let yourself down.
There is a home, where you
find space amidst hostility.
A home with four chambers.
One tiny broken heart,
And they called it heart wreckage.

Corrupted!
When it all collapsed,
a terror passed through her mind.
It was an abrupt end.
Yet, a new episode began.
She dwelled on the fragments,
Enclosed with corrupted signals
Too long to be awakened.
Slowly, falling apart
In a curious world
Coping to hold the breath
Gradually tuning to infinite resonances.
Moving from the far edges
Breaking down!!!
Her heart surpassed the wreckage
Nonetheless, her mind carried it
And modified the self.
Now, with the altered self,
her psyche is struggling to decode
the utterances.
All the signals from the brain
are encrypted to the core.
Resulting in a super new 'modified self'.

Back Ashore

I was diving deep
Dark as the cavernous eyes
I was diving into the depths
A straight dive into the wreck.
Slowly, conquering a vast blue ocean.
When the days of despair were over,
I heard a distant cry.
And those haunting melancholic eyes
shed tears.
Gradually moving back ashore
I could only recollect tales
told from the days of yore.
Reminiscences of the great wreckage.

Pieces
Oh, this brooding darkness
Is creeping everywhere.
With lurking fears, I'm
Ravaged to pieces.
Amidst worries, I become
More and more anxious.
While in this chaotic cycle
Of panic attacks,
I shriek inside,
And I am lost to infinity.

Parting
As time flew by,
Nothing got mended.
Instead, a vast void was formed
Lover's heart turned to a haunting desert.
She failed to withstand,
The burning heat of longing...
Forgiving is hard,
Forgetting is harder.
As time flew by,
Nothing was mended
And nothing remained the same
At the end,
The heart whispered
Adieu, my love.

Reflections

I

She took a mirror and looked into it
It reflected her face
She saw a broken image.
Oblivion called her name
She jumped into the sea
The water dissolved her image
Waves licked her marks clean
Like a leaf,
she withered away from the world.

II

Life –
A shattered story
Unable to recollect
A forlorn past
With broken memories
And the search for meaning
Lie hidden
beneath the layer
between sane and insane moments.

Confession
Submerged in the chaotic waves
A feeble sigh is heard.
Suddenly a great void,
encircles the heart
Resulting in the overflow of tears.
A huge image is shattered
Several pieces,
floated on the surface of memory
Some reach ashore
Slowly the stony heart,
turns to flesh
Giving birth to new life.

Voyage of Discovery
When will this journey of chaos end?
All these years,
I have been searching
for something deep inside.
Like maggots,
fear and anxiety attacked my inner self,
And ruined my courage.
Now in great agony, I live tormented
Tossed between cleaved
soul and flesh.
I carry an unhappy heart inside
Follow your heart, they say
I tried hard to convince myself
It was strange when my emotions
crossed the borders of my body
I was uncertain about my feelings
I felt like an abandoned soul,
with a broken heart.
Slowly, I gather the courage
to express my real self,
buried for long years; not anymore!
Too stagnated in the gutters
of confusion and chaos.
I recognized a soul in this suffocating body
My quest for finding the real me
trapped in the wrong body reached the peak
And here begins the voyage,
The real voyage of discovery.

Forsaken

Weeping near the desolate valley
I found no one to console me.
Overflowing tears, blurred vision!
Now, on the edge of helplessness.
Like an abandoned soul, life drifts
Without a shore to take dwelling.
And the very thought of existence,
Reflects the homeless heart.

Choking Under the Voices
Oh! that first heartfelt experience
of affront and humiliation
Tormented the psyche for several days
To shun the rememberings of agony,
eyes shed tears for long days
And the rain continued for a week
The voices of teasing
echoed in her mind
Slowly she doomed herself into a long hush
And started to gasp the anguish
that came along her way
It continued
Till the thoughts blasted.
Gradually she started to hear
the voices of monster
All the scathing bouts echoed
again and again with a powerful tempo
From dawn to dusk,
it annoyed her sanity
The monster proceeded to rise and recede
Suddenly, she felt the whole life
emerging like an abandoned kite
From scorching thoughts to dark
and stormy moods,
shades of life changed.
In the end, one question started to
whimper in her mind
Whom should she blame?
Her abusers or the poor brain
that got altered in the entire turmoil
that came along her way?

Fragmented Piece of Word
The unspeakable moments
The unspeakable truth
The self, shattered and fragmented
The words dissolved deep in her heart
And she uttered
a fragmented piece of word
The buried piece of the fragmented word
created greater chaos and agony inside
The unspeakable moments
created an unspeakable truth
The unspeakable truth
created an untold story
Untold story fragmented
into pieces of words.
In the end,
her heart bore witness
to the story
of
that
fragmented
piece
of
word.

Burial
The ceremony had ended
All had left
Wandering in the last
Night's lost thoughts
All she found was a little grit
Wrapped in a thin layer of hope.
Concealed to the core
Drenched in the unfathomed emotions
Now, a mere ghost
Has arisen from a forlorn past
Haunts the soul like a nightmare
When the continuous rain ended
There completed the ceremony
And the ghost vanished.

Drowning
Floating on the fathomless water
With empty heart
Longing for an ancient love
Years of waiting doesn't dim
the light inside.
Moon smiled, whispered a secret
Slowly, empty heart weighed heavy
And drowned in the fathomless water.
Soul transcends
Oh! Eternal bliss
You make the soul sunshine.

Buried Pangs
She buried her sorrows
in the fathomless depths of her heart.
Overwhelmed by thoughts
Lost in tears
Her soul scalded
Unable to explain.
As an aftermath of engulfing the whole pain
Her eyes detained a new story, yet to be told.
Hidden truths struggled within
Whole world seemed too hostile.
She became an abandoned soul
With a broken heart.
In the end, she died
One piece at a time.

Stains of Stigma
Once a wandering weary soul was I
Too lost in the airless spaces
With a tiny wavering heart,
I searched for lost thoughts.
Alas! My realm sunk in the dreary ocean
Unable to breathe under the starry sky
Little by little, it disappeared.
From the far edges of psyche,
Now, a vague image can be seen.
A terrified isolated cry was echoed
Poor soul, too tired of the prejudices
It's your fault, it's your fault!
Words cling to the deep core.
Stained with stigma
Unable to utter
Soul drained, body collapsed
A great turmoil,
A dark abyss!

She Writer
She travelled,
through the narrow corridors
of her psyche
Through the deep
realms of her mind
Too tired,
fears numbed her senses
She mumbled a few words
Whacked, cracked, and wracked
She felt completely burnt out
Some said she is mad
"Beware of a woman,
who writes and reads a lot"
"It can even cause
a mental breakdown"
She felt like a prisoner
of the prejudiced world
Stained with ink
Words bled,
filled the blank pieces of paper
There she found her voice
Found her, self again
Slowly, endowed with strength
She confessed,
The innermost vibes of her heart
When reality struck her with a
pointed knife,
She closed the doors of outer world
Explored the inner realms of life.
To breathe the fresh air of hope,
she builds a room of her own.

Twinges of Sorrow

These are those pangs,
buried deep in our heart.
One day, it will find a way
Through the cracks.
Oh! Pangs of distress...
I stood near the closed door and wept
Then, found a desolate valley
Where I could roam ceaselessly.
Oh! Pangs of guilt...
I was too lost in the burning fire
Engulfed by the heat.
Slowly, submerged in the twinges of sorrow
Too lost to be found again!

A Poem on Grief and Love
At the end of a chapter,
You mourn
Because it's the final chapter
Book closed.
Nothing more, nothing less.
Life, characters, lessons
All became stories
Forlorn past troubles my tiny heart
My mind, drenched in sorrowful angst
My soul aches.
Oh! My soul's greatest loss
How dearly I loved thee
Thou withered away like a leaf
Nothing can set me apart from your fond memories.
New roots sprout in my mind
Tiny flowers bloom in my heart's chamber.
With everlasting fragrance.
Oh! Love
Thou kindle my soul
Thy memories are sweet melody
That makes my heart alive.

Unsaid

These days,
I have been thinking about words.
Yes, the power of words.
There is magic in every word,
that is spoken with kindness.
I wonder what happens
to those unuttered words.
They reach your throat,
but you swallowed them out of fear.
A great loss!
Else, you saved a heart
from its destined wreckage.
Some words float,
on the surface of memory
Slowly, dissolving to taste sour.
Those unsaid words
become a great regret.
Leaving behind a great void.
And nothing will suffice
to fill its emptiness.

Pondering Over Love
I was preoccupied in a quest for meaning.
In a world filled with chaos,
Slowly I started to disappear in the memories.
Memories of bygone love.
I have entered the days of yore.
While trying to figure out the truth,
Whether I have lived deeply
To receive the greatest heartbreak.
And reconciling with my past self,
I am looking forward to accepting
The fate of getting more heart wreckage.
Life is filled with tints of sadness and happiness.
And, the curse of experiencing
wreckage is undeniable.
Yes, I was deeply engulfed in the search for meaning.
In the ashes of bygone love!
Little by little,
I will fade away in the wild tears.

Love, Again & Again
I have taken a pen to write down my thoughts.
The thoughts that passed through my troubled mind,
to make it more troublesome.
And I started to worry about it.
Let's write and think about love.
My tiny heart whispered.
I know, one day
love will conquer my whole heart.
And will become my whole.
How much love has been wasted in vain
By not even taking any effort
To kindle its warmth and affection.
Love that was wasted,
will never return to you
with the same passion and affection
that it was once filled with.
Its reciprocity is unpredictable.
Either you will feel its chill and numbness
Or you will feel the warmth and wellness
That it brings.
If there is no love,
You will feel the whole strangeness in that stranger.
Aah! They loved love more than the lover.
They loved words more than the writer.
They loved being loved
But never bothered to love at all!
To love,
is to start a vigorous and daring journey.
To love is to give what you have.
To love is to break the door of self
And to take what it provides.

Yes, to love is to break and bleed
Unto the last drop from its core.

To My Homeless Heart
Dear, you are holding too much
than you can carry.
You are bearing too much
than you can endure.
I will write the most melancholic songs...
Otherwise, I will sink into the depths of despair!
My home and I are now too far apart.
The home where I took refuge
And my room where I shed tears
Now seem to be symbols of solitude.
It smells of my cluttered thoughts and wet tears.
Here, I remember much better.
About the sad and shocking past.
And I will be reminded
of the raw realities and future.
Here we go... into the home!
Raised in the five-member family
We three never made a home.
We were all all-alone than together.
The eldest and the firstborn,
Ceased living when she was too young!
Now she lives in another world
Where sometimes she completely loses herself.
We are sisters; but trust me I am alone!
Middle one, that's me
Led a life in between.
Younger one, the brother
His world is more coloured than mine.
We are under one roof,
But trust me I am alone!
And I failed to find a home in their hearts.

Into the Heart
I am searching for a little
space to breathe
Because you shun me
from the corridors of your heart.
I believe love is magic,
that changes you entirely
and makes you a new being.
I can't count the distance
to your heart,
But I can feel each
throb of your heart.
When two hearts unite,
there begins a journey
A long journey filled with
huddles of sadness and struggles.
Give me a little space to breathe.
They say it's hard to believe one,
I know, when trust is shaken,
nothing can mend the broken pieces.
Let's begin a new journey
I can't promise you,
roses without thorns
and a haven without desert.
Let's begin a journey,
a journey to each other's heart
Let's delve deep and plant
the seeds of hope and trust.
Let it bloom eternally
And never let the burning sun
fade the light of trust inside.

Outcaste

Silenced for years...
Relegated to the fringes of society
Ignored and excluded for centuries
Now, we live on the peripheries.
Oh! Oppression...
You raise your hands
Everywhere...we're denied freedom
Yes! We are the untouchable ones!!
Years of struggles, sorrows, and tears
Shattered our voice
Scattered our lives.
Oh! that experience of discrimination,
burned our body and soul.
Failing to withstand
the burning heat of your wrath,
We jumped into the sea of oblivion.
For years, we lived leaving no trace.
Marginalized in every sphere
Subjugated in the name of
dark colour, inferior caste,
race and gender.
You called us outcasts.
We can't bear this injustice anymore...
We will take our ink-dipped swords.
Speak out our truths
Write our stories
To mark our discontent.

Tomorrow's Sky
Amidst the chaos,
there arose a star
at the topmost corner of the sky.
Oh! Uncertain times,
when I lost patience,
my heart shrunken
my troubled faith
became my great weakness.
I questioned thee
I moaned that your
plans caused my downfall.
Like a stone, you stood,
my poor heart thought.
When dark clouds fade,
the sky slowly becomes clear.
Once,
I counted my life lost
my dreams dead.
Oh! Eternal love, you saved
my soul from wretched fears
and thy words lifted my whole life
from the abysm of darkness.
Thy light like the sun, shined
in tomorrow's sky brighter than ever.

Life Journeys
At every juncture,
you have to choose your way
At every crossroad,
you have to take your turn
At every crucial moment
you have to take your decision
After every heartbreak,
you have to move on
After every failure
you have to let it go.
Life is a cycle of journeys
You can't cling to a particular path,
When one journey ends, another begins.
When one cycle ends, another starts,
From birth to death, cycle of life repeats.
Some journeys end painful
Some are hopeful
Some are delightful
A journey to the interior is a must
to find the real you.
Choose your path,
and dare to begin the journey.
It will make a huge change in life
and you will never be the same.

A Way to Lost Thoughts
Dear,
It's hard to dig deep
and find the thoughts lost in despair...
When mind becomes blurred,
to clear the vision
Outpour the dark clouds
that surround your heart
Breathe out all the toxic air
Breathe in the air of hope
And reignite the spark in your eyes
All that you had lost once
Are not lost forever
When the clouds of Chaos move out
You will definitely find a way
To your lost thoughts...

Gentle Reminder

I

At this youthful and vigorous age,
When you count the heartbreaks
It will not suffice your longings to find love.
Let yourself feel the weight of lonely days and nights.
Let yourself feel the pain of longing.
Let your soul find your love.
Ah! To live devoid of love,
Seems to be heavy and hard.
Let your emotions slowly reach your heart.
Don't repress it.
Longings and heartbreaks will make you alive inside.
Let your heart break when you feel sad.
In the end, only heartbreaks count.
That is how many lives you have lived.

II

In life, meant to be lived,
It truly matters, what lasts and what doesn't.
Dear,
Don't compare your tiny young self with others.
You have a different story to tell.
That's your unique tale.
Our unique tale is woven
in the mysteries of sorrows and agony.
Only you know, how you have survived
the cold tears and burning heat of life.
You are moulded in a way
to embrace the raw realities of life.

Irrecoverable
All hope fails to find the reason.
An irrecoverable loss!
When you sense that there were only absences.
To intensify your feelings,
There exists no passion
Nor true emotions
Then a great realization
will be stuck in your mind.
No love! Not at all!
The question to reconcile
will disappear slowly.
And you will gradually dissolve
in the disillusioned teardrops.
Unrecoverable damage!

Creed on Love
I do believe in love,
Even if
I don't carry another heart.
I do believe in love,
Even if
Love is a word that stands far from me.
Yes, I do believe in love,
because love is stronger than death.
And here is,
my small yet
powerful creed on love
Which I keep holding on to.

Holding On
Now, I will write.
So, the comeback will be easier.
There is a language,
Unknown to the universe,
Where you connect with the Creator.
Suffering is the price,
We have paid,
to open the door.

A Life to Live
Sometimes,
You swim through turbulent waves
Some days,
You hit rock bottoms.
When life leads you to the dull shores,
Dear, don't let yourself down.
There will come a day,
You realize the power of trust and hope
The most beautiful things to hold on to.
Remember, this is your life
A life to live.

Toxic Positivity
Alas! Your words couldn't save a heart
from its wreckage!
When your words failed to give hope
To a broken heart,
And your life seemed too good to be true,
One couldn't appreciate it.
When your thoughts clashed in their psyche,
They thought that you were a fake being,
Selling motivation and inspiration
But you utterly failed to carry the light
And hold hope.
Finally, they called you toxic
And expelled from their realm.

Cursed Lives
Sometimes, suffering means sacrifices.
I wonder,
Why suffering comes in the form of illness.
In no way could I find it a blessing.
But, when you have to endure certain pain,
that comes into your life
as an uninvited friend
Or as a stranger,
You are forced to bear it.
There is no way out.
Some lives are considered cursed
Specially those wrapped
in thin layers of disability.
Sometimes it will be evident
Else, the layer will be too thin
To be discovered in the early stages.
Some hearts and minds are prone
To the tragic flow of events
When these vulnerable minds
get exposed to tragedies
Some become totally melancholic,
Others partially.
We tend to call these lives cursed.
But those tiny poor hearts
Are made of melancholic
songs and souls.
And their lives are sung
by some melancholic muse.
Cursed they may be deemed
But they are never doomed!

Autumn Blues
Autumn reminds me of many.
From yellow to brown,
Leaves are going through a process.
Of withering.
Withering away is an art.
Slowly disappearing,
As the meaning says.
In a fast-pacing world it's not that easy.
The blues are not bright.
When autumn strikes,
What if blues accompany us?
Nobody can escape.
Sorrow is a big river,
Teeming with dead dreams
And unaccomplished wishes.
Its shores are strewn
with forgotten thoughts.
Sadly, sorrows are part of our lives.
Nobody can promise us life,
without sorrowful days.
When blues hit us in autumn,
Slowly it crouches
Into our thoughts.
When it slowly reaches the heart,
The heart pumps out blue
Instead of red!
And blue, dull years ahead...

Battle Field

I will greet you,
On the finest morning
With my whole heart.
I will meet you on the battlefield.
Where you battered,
between right and wrong.
I will come to seek shelter for you
From the biting wind.
There, I will be your refuge.
When you travel through wavering waves,
I will teach you how to dance.
I will listen to your ruined musings
and old bragging.
I will seek you
in the broken-down pasture.
Where you died piece by piece.
And, I will sing a song among lilacs
In the old valley of sorrows.

Slaughtered Thoughts
Dear life, I don't wish
Simple or happy days to lead.
When life turns,
It turns out to be a messy room.
Where you cannot find anything in order.
You can't blame others for everything.
There will come a day you realize
You have to be responsible
For the irresponsible twists and turns of life.
You have to be more courageous than ever!
Ordinary days have already gone.
I'm not counting the bygone nights.
When memories flash in your mind,
Be steady like a commander
Who orders to slay the foe.
When unwanted thoughts intrude
Like an uninvited acquaintance
You can welcome, them with half mind.
Or you can slaughter them like an animal.
Ahh! Slaughtered thoughts...
Where will you bury them!
Where will you hide its remnants?
There is nothing more sinister
Than slaughtering thoughts.
To kill inch by inch, sans mercy.
If you have done it,
Then great!
You can hide the blood
In the dark corner of your heart.
But the stains will remain
To corrode your mind forever.

On Patience
I will wait
Until the last word
Conquers and illumes
The unlit world.
I will write
Until the final page
Lifts the soul from despair.
With patience
I will hold back
The tears.
Once I was dealing in
desperate days
of longing.
In those days
of utter confusion
I was battered
Between choices.
I heard a distant song
That echoed in my heart.
"The sun will rise again".
I woke up
From the dark days
To greet the dawn.

Haunted House
Moving through the aisles,
Door to door.
Ghost figures, we are.
Hiding from daylight
Awake the whole night
Searching for unconquered lives.
Haunted by grave memories
We sing songs from an unknown past.
And swing with renderings
Of unsung songs from life.
To future, we are unknown beings
To have ceased living before dawn.
We are unborn ones
Cursed to live in this haunted house.
We are homeless beings
With shattered dreams
And hopeless cries
Echoing from distant hills.
We roam seamlessly
from past to future.
Without knowing the truth.
Hiding from rainy days
and autumn evenings.
We were rooted in utmost longings.
We were cursed,
to live in utter darkness.
We were cursed to live among ghosts.
We lost all our hope.
We live homeless,
In this haunted house.

On Purpose
We can't live many lives
That's true.
But we can renew our lives.
Trees in the autumn
Shed leaves
to welcome the new season.
Never let your sorrows
Drain you.
Never let your setbacks
Stumble you.
And never let your doubts
Conquer you.
One life,
with many aspirations.
One day,
to make the change.
One decision,
to challenge the unchallenged.
One life,
to motivate many lives.
Maybe yours will not be a success story.
But you can be true to yourself
Then yours will be a true story.
A story to be rendered.
Yes, you are here
To lead a life of purpose.

Ageing
Do our sorrows and pains
Fade away when we grow up?
Do our dreams outgrow
Our past disappointments?
With ageing
Nothing changes, except the body.
We wish to become more mature.
But our wounded self
Acts childishly each time
To disgrace us.
We are rooted in yesterday's sorrows.
Out of anguish, a big tree grows
And its fruits are full of lifeless essence.
Can we outgrow the despair
Of the upcoming days?
Can we foresee the shining stars
In the sky?
Without accepting the heartache
We cannot dream of tomorrow's sky.

Walking Barefoot
To walk barefoot
Through fire
Is inexplicable.
When you have moved
Some inches
From the border
Of sanity
You will feel like
You have been trapped
In airless spaces.
And you get lost to obscurity
It's a one-way ticket
You won't buy it again
Later, you will regret
Buying it.
At some point
You recognize that
You have travelled so far
All barefoot.
You will get the shock of your life
When you realise
How hard the journey was.
Because you have fought the war
barehanded
And walked every step
Barefooted.

Exit

My sky is full of exits.
When wounds disappear,
Slowly scars become visible.
Out of the memories
From the battlefield
A battered self originates.
Here I am
I will wait
Until the last remnant dissolves
Into the remains of the day.
Yes, I believe
Grace abounds
And doors are open.
I exist.

www.ingramcontent.com/pod-product-compliance
Lightning Source LLC
Chambersburg PA
CBHW021347160726
47994CB00007B/2874